MW00633187

Healing
Hands

MARILYN DIANE GRENION C.

ISBN 978-1-0980-0804-8 (paperback)
ISBN 978-1-0980-1469-8 (hardcover)
ISBN 978-1-0980-0805-5 (digital)

Christian Faith Publishing, Inc.
832 Park Avenue
Meadville, PA 16335
www.christianfaithpublishing.com

Printed in the United States of America

Father, in the name of Jesus, I thank you for your love, your goodness, your mercy, and your grace. Thank you for illuminating the dark areas of my life and giving me sight. I ask for your forgiveness for denying Christ and refusing to walk in my true identity as a daughter of the King.

I receive your forgiveness, knowing that I and my Father are one and I have no life outside of you. Therefore, I now make a conscious decision to acknowledge you in all of my ways, knowing that you will direct my path in completing this book that I started so long ago.

I dedicate this book to my very kind and loving husband, my two sons that God has given me the honor to birth and bring into my experience, to my six siblings, to all of my grandchildren, and to my two stepchildren. I love you all. To my mother, may God continue to shower his blessings upon you, and most of all, to my dear friends who have been waiting to read it.

Endorsements

This is a story of redemptive love: God's love for Marilyn; Marilyn's love for herself and her neighbor as herself! This is a journey of vulnerability and candor, of self-acceptance and peace, and of finding true self-worth. Women, men, and children will read this story, experience this love, participate in the journey, and find wholeness.

This story shows how God makes no mistakes and how he uses every situation of our lives to create beauty out of ashes. A must read for the empowerment of the soul!

—Betsie Green
NYC educator

As I read this manuscript, two things became obvious (1) struggles, though painful at times are used by God to help us become mature believers in Christ and (2) true fulfillment is only possible after we discover His purpose for our lives and begin the journey by faith to accomplish that purpose. Written from the heart, its contents will resonate with many and bring them the encouragement that comes from knowing that the God who brought Marilyn out is no respecter of persons.

—Lincoln Joseph
Sunday school teacher/aviation instructor

Contents

1. Remembrance 11

2. God Wants My Attention....................................18

3. God Has My Attention 21

4. Tithes and Offering..25

5. Transition..30

6. Where Is My Wealth? 36

7. The Grasshopper Complex..................................41

8. Get Your Self-esteem Off the Seesaw 42

9. My Mother, My Friend 44

10. The Wise Use of Money.....................................45

11. Are You Eclipsing Your Growth by Your Thinking? 47

12. Is There Room in You for the Christ Child? 49

13. It Shall Cost You 51

14. Children Live What They Learn, but I Am No
    Longer a Child...53

15. How Do You See Yourself? 55

16. Finding Balance...57

17. Family or Foe 59

Original poems from my *Rivers of Life* collection.........................61

I made my entrance into the world on May 18, 1959 in a small village (now a town) named Bartica. Bartica is situated in the only English-speaking country named Guyana in South America a.k.a. Land of Many Waters. I am the fourth child in a family of seven children. As I reflect on the early years of my life, I can now do so with joyful anticipation of what I am yet to discover about myself. A few years ago, I had attempted to write after receiving a prophetic word of being a writer what I thought was my whole life story, but even as I began to put pen on paper, I knew in my spirit that was not the truth concerning me. What I had written was all of the unpleasant memories of the experiences I've had in my childhood and early adulthood and it was toxic and full of bitterness, anger, and resentment. I sensed that Holy Spirit was telling me that if anyone had read what I had written, it would not have helped or blessed them in any way, especially if they had similar experiences like I did that they wanted to overcome. Therefore, I trashed it. He told me that one day I was going to write it again, but from another perspective and mindset because whoever reads it would have to see where I've been and how I was able to become an overcomer. Now I know that the experiences I've had so far in my life was either God-willed or allowed for His glory.

I tried a few years later, but I had only written the outline, according to my lovely friend, Margaret C. So now, I have added the content.

Another prophetic word that I received years ago was "I see you as a rose being crushed by a giant's footstep, but God." I know for the fragrance to come out of a flower it must be crushed. There are synthetic fragrances created by putting chemicals together and are not very costly, and there are fragrances made from crushed flowers, scented wood, fruits, spices, and herbs—all authentic ingredients created only by Almighty God—and are very costly. I remember a long time after getting that word at the church where I was a member at the time, the pastor encouraged the members to bring our own bottle of oil to have it blessed for praying and anointing purposes. I took my oil up, had it blessed, and went back to my seat. I then noticed a sister in Christ went up twice but the second time, she had a bottle of perfume in her hand. After getting it blessed, she came to me and said, "God told me to give this to you."

I pray that the essence of my life will be a sweet-smelling fragrance in the nostrils of my Heavenly Father. Thank you for giving me beauty for ashes and the oil of joy for my sorrows.

1

Remembrance

As far as I can remember, I had two loving parents. I used the word had because my father is now deceased. At the tender age of three years old, unfortunately, my parents separated. As I grew older, I've heard many conflicting stories of what caused their separation, but being married for almost thirty-eight years and learning from my own experience, I know that for any marriage relationship to last, it takes so much more than two people saying I love you to have a successful marriage. There should be serious conversations about each other's background, family history, how to handle conflict, having and raising children, finances, spirituality, cultural differences, and relationship with extended family members. I know that some things can only be learned while being married and living together, but it would also be wise to seek counseling from someone who knows how to ask the hard questions. I used to say that I did not have good role models of what it means to have a successful marriage among most of the people who helped to raise me, but I have changed that. They have indirectly taught me what not to do. When someone say I love you, they just may be talking about passionate or romantic love (Eros). According to 1 Corinthians 13:4–5 (KJV), "Charity suffereth long, and is kind; charity envieth not; charity vaunteth not itself, is not puffed up, doth not behave itself unseemly, seeketh not her own, it is not easily provoked, thinketh no evil." That is the God kind of love.

I was the only girl among three brothers, two older and one younger than I. My mother left us in the care of our maternal grandmother and our father. Dad spent a lot of time working and away from home but made sure we were provided for financially. He would leave open accounts in a few stores in the village where my grandmother or an older female cousin, who also lived with my grandmother, could have gone and gotten supplies that we needed. Upon his fortnightly or monthly return, he would go to the creditors and pay his bills.

There were also stepmothers, an aunt, and a family friend who were a part of my life, if not my brothers, and also a lot of movement in terms of where I lived that interrupted my education. Between the age of six and seven years old, my father separated me from my brothers and took me to live with one of his relatives in the city because he was not happy about the way I was being treated where I was. My introduction to that house was quite traumatic. A little girl, a few years older than I, invited me to go outside with her to play. She then picked a hot pepper from their kitchen garden, smashed it, and rubbed it in my face. My face was on fire and I was terrified. Our parents ran outside to investigate what the noise was about, and she told them, when she heard that I was coming there to live, she thought that I was a little baby not almost as old as her and that was her reason for smashing the pepper and rubbing it in my face. I am sure that my father must have thought that he made a mistake to bring me there, but I do not know what other options he had. After a little while, my youngest brother joined me and I was happy to see a familiar face, but now there was not just one unwelcomed kid to abuse but two by the two youngest children in the house. They were relentless with their insults and physical abuse, calling us out of our names and telling lies on us, which most times got us in trouble. I was also sexually molested by an older person who was always seemingly "nice" to me. Children need to know that molesters can appear to be nice and kind in order to gain their trust. Did I tell anyone? No, did not know I was supposed to tell and who was going to believe me anyway.

Our mother found out that we were living in the city and she came to visit us. Before leaving, she promised that she will be back shortly to get us and she did. We went to live with her and our two younger sisters born after she and my father had separated. My two older brothers also came to join us. That was the only time that I can remember that all six siblings were together under one roof. I want to also acknowledge that later in my teenage years, my father told me that he had another daughter; therefore, I now have six siblings. Life was not good for my mother financially, so our little family reunion was short lived. My two older brothers went back to live with my grandmother, my youngest brother and I were left with an older cousin who was married and living in the same house with us, and Mom took the two smaller children with her to a faraway village where she found work. Shortly after, our cousin who was pregnant and soon to giving birth, packed up her two existing children and went back to my grandmother and my youngest brother and I were left without any adult supervision and food for a couple of days. This was not the first time that my youngest brother and I were left alone to fend for ourselves. The first time, we were abandoned by a step-mother and we had to find our way to our grandmother's house. God must have been looking out for us because two days later my cousin's husband came home from the army and was surprised and upset to find my brother and I hungry and alone. Our resquer in shining armor cooked and fed us and promised that he will not leave until he got in contact with our mother, and that is exactly what he did. Mom came home and sent my youngest brother back to my grand-mother, then placed my two sisters and I with a family friend whom we fondly called Granny, then went back to work. Memories of this home are pleasant for me in comparison to the other homes where I lived during my early childhood and young adulthood. Granny was a disciplinarian, but also very kind. She had a granddaughter living with her who was a few years older than me that I am still friends with today. A few years ago, I met her in Barbados and we reminisced about old days, and I reminded her of how well we got along when my sisters and I lived with her and her grandmother. She said, "My grandmother would not have had it any other way." My mother would come to see my sisters and I on her days off, but eventually she left the job and came and removed us from Granny's house. I was sent to live with the same cousin who left my brother and I alone in the house. In defense of my cousin, she was pregnant and ready to give birth and she needed our grandmother's help, so off she went. I do not know if she had a contact number for my mother, and my brother and I were not her responsibility anyway. I recently found out that I was sent to live at her house because that is where my father chose to send my financial support. Life just became a little more difficult for me. I was never into sports because coming home with a smudge on my clothes was a problem; therefore, I always sat on the sidelines as a spectator and not a participator and had no friends. Now I know how much fun and games are important to a child's development. This is where you learn teamwork and how to be a team player, building confidence, willing to try new things, and overcoming fears.

As an adult, I was perceived by some of being mean because I would not smile, always had a serious look on my face, and did not know how to laugh at a joke. I was even told by a pastor that I needed to go to an amusement park and have some fun. I did but I still sat on the sideline. It was just in recent years when my first granddaughter asked her father if Grandma Marilyn don't smile, also my second granddaughter would remind me to smile by asking, "Grandma, why are you not smiling?" That made me very sad because I want my grandchildren to see the happiness, joy, and delight, expressed on my face whenever we see each other because I love them so much. So, I bought a cup with a smiley face to remind myself to smile every time I drink out of it.

At the young age of fifty-nine years in 2018, I had the most fun ever, spending Christmas holiday with my oldest son and his lovely family in Minnesota. My granddaughter convinced me to go tubing down the icy slopes, and I must admit that I enjoyed myself so much that I did it five or six times. I thank God for allowing me to have that wonderful experience of fun and play even two generations later.

I loved singing, drawing, and poetry, and those were some of the things that I looked forward to on Fridays. I would be kept at home to babysit while my cousin and her friend would go to the city. One Friday after my cousin had left, I was looking out of a window and an elderly neighbor saw me and asked why almost every Friday I was at home and not in school? She became very upset after I told her I had to babysit. She then told me to bring the baby over to her house and promised that she will speak to my cousin when she returned, and that I should go to school. I was excited and afraid at the same time. It was a rainy day, and on my way down the stairs, I slipped and fell. The baby rolled down the steps and I fell off the side. When I stood up, my back was a little sore and the baby was crying. After I picked him up, he immediately stopped crying. I guess I had bundled him up so well to prevent the rain from wetting him that he did not get hurt, but I was even more afraid of the wrath of my cousin. The neighbor assured me that all would be well. When I returned from school, my cousin was at home but not a word concerning the incident was ever mentioned to me and I was never kept away from school on Fridays again.

There was no lack of mental, verbal, and physical abuse. My oldest brother came just in time one day and saved me from being beaten over my head with an army boot after I was accused of breaking off the freezer door. I got my head slammed down on the top of the refrigerator, which resulted in my face being busted. A few years ago, she told me how sorry she was for busting my face, and I then had the opportunity to explain to her for the first time, how the freezer door fell off because she was now listening. She turned off the heavily-frosted refrigerator and told me to clean it when I got home from school, and when I opened the outer door of the refrigerator, all of the ice had melted and the freezer door fell off. It must have been that the built-up ice had pushed the door off the hinges. I was glad that she apologized for her sake because I was not holding any grudges against her. Sad to say, but sometimes, the people who are supposed to love and take care of you are the same people who say and do the most cruel things to you. Many times, I was told by family members that I was a nobody, will not amount to much, and where I will end up on the scale of life, but now that I am an adult and have more understanding, I've learned that according to Ephesians 6:12 (KJV), "For we wrestle not against flesh and blood but principalities and powers and spiritual wickedness in high places." Flesh and blood are not our enemy. Hurt people can only give you what they have and that is their pain. I know for sure that my cousin had her own hurts and disappointments in her life and needed help for herself.

I was now living with my mother again and attending a private high school in the city. My self-esteem was so low and I felt like my life was an out-of-control roller coaster. I was constantly being called into the school office for nonpayment or late payment of my school fees because the money coming from my father was sure to come but sometimes late because of the location where he was working. It became very difficult for me to concentrate on my school work. One day, I had gotten thrown out of the class, not for being rude or disrespectful, but for being totally zoned out and not being able to answer the teacher's questions. Now I realized that I must have been depressed. In those days, if anyone had asked me how I was doing, I do not think that I would have had the words to articulate what I was experiencing. I dropped out of school and went back to my father and a step mother who did not appear to be happy when my brothers and I were around, then back to my mother again, and enrolled in a business school to take a course in shorthand, typewriting, and English. That is where I managed to obtain an Advanced English diploma. I guess God was preparing me to write this book.

Before going any further, I want to pause and give honor where honor is due according to Romans 13:7. First, I want to thank God for keeping me through the years of vulnerability and uncertainty. Also, for the people who were there for me as a child, even for those who were like sandpaper, thank you for smoothing out the rough places in my life. It was sometimes very painful but I guess necessary. As it is written in 1 Peter 1:6-7 (KJV), "Wherein ye greatly rejoice, though now for a season, if need be, ye are in heaviness through manifold temptation. That the trial of your faith being much more precious than of gold that perisheth, though it be tried with fire, might be found unto praise and honor and glory at the appearing of Jesus Christ." Thanks also to my now-deceased grandmother who lived to be almost 104 years old. Also, to my cousin. They both did their best with the knowledge that they had and what was available to them. Thanks to the Obermuller children who shared their home and their mother with me. Their home was a place of peace, love, and comfort whenever I had the opportunity to visit, even though they did not know it at the time as I've been told by some of the children.

2

God Wants My Attention

I met my husband for the first time on my seventeenth birthday at the home of my mother's friend, and we started dating some time later. I was so needy for love, attention, friendship, and stability that by the age of twenty, I became pregnant with my first son. At three months pregnant, the father of my child who is now my husband, travelled to the USA on a scholarship to attend school, and my mother left a month later also for the USA, seeking a better life for herself and her children. When the father of my child returned to Guyana, our son was eight months old. He had made the promise that if I waited for him he would come back and we will get married. Well, I waited, he came back, and we got married.

I started to come into serious parental maturity after my son had a few mishaps. Early one morning, I had taken him with me to the window to see his father off to work and must have left the window unlocked, went back to bed with him, and feel asleep. I was dreaming that someone gave me three eggs and one fell out of my hand on to a table, rolled off of the table, and then broke. I woke up to the loud calling of my neighbor. I did not see my baby on the bed or in the bedroom, so I ran frantically outside to the living room but he was not there either. I opened the door and there was my neighbor who lived on the first floor of the two-story house where we lived, holding and shaking my baby in her arms. He was ten months old and very active and must have pushed the chair up to the window and climbed up for the first time and fell out. Miraculously, he did not have a bump, bruise, or scratch on his body. I took him to the emergency room and the doctor told me to just keep him quiet. There were no laws at the time that I was aware of that required a landlord to place child safety bars on the windows. A few months later, he became ill and had to be hospitalized. Lots of babies were getting sick with a gastrointestinal water-borne disease. After being in the hospital for a couple of days, he was discharged but got sick again, in spite of all of the precautions I was now taking by boiling the water for everything that I did for him. I was utterly perplexed at this point. I ran into two Christian young women who lived across the street from us, and I told them about the troubles I was having with my son's health. They encouraged me to bring him to their place of worship that night and to believe God for his healing. Well I did, I must admit out of desperation, and he got better. Shortly after, we moved into another house and here came trouble again. He started complaining of a pulling in his face and his speech was sometimes slurred. I had taken him to several doctors but nothing changed. One of the doctors asked me if his father spent quality time with him. I guess that he was trying to see if there was something psychological happening, and the other question was did I give him vitamins. I had even mentioned the fall that he had earlier but they had no diagnosis for his condition. He was missing school quite a lot, and I was scared and fearing the worst for his life.

I heard as a child from one of my aunts of Proverbs 22:6 (KJV), "Train up a child in the way he should go: and when he is old, he will not depart from it." I guess that's why I thought it was right for me to send him to church and Sunday school, but how right was I, if I was not taking him myself, I always had an excuse—I do not have church clothes or I do not have the time. Those were just lies. He would be taught Bible verses and then come home and ask me to find the verses in the Bible. Sad to say, I did not have a Bible. May God rest the soul of Miss Ronnie who would come over with her gigantic Bible and search out the scripture for my little boy. Sometimes, he would be playing outside on the steps and I could hear him preaching. Once, I asked him who he was preaching to and his answer was to the little birdies that flew by. I am smiling as I write this because it warms my heart.

After I started attending church with him, I heard the pastor asking the question, "Whose duty it is to bring up the child in the fear of the Lord? Is it the church or the parents?" Obviously, it is the parents.

3

God Has My Attention

I began having dreams of God speaking to me and at one time when I was out in a night club partying with my husband. We were not party animals, but occasionally, we would go out to celebrate our wedding anniversary or birthdays. We had secured our son with a babysitter, got dressed (remember I said before I had no church clothes) and as we were leaving out of the door, my son placed his little arms around my neck and pleaded with me to take him to church the next day. I told him yes, I would, but I had no intention of doing so. My husband and I were never drinkers or smokers, but we loved to dance. It seemed like most people in the club were drinking, smoking, dancing, and having a good time except us because we were being suffocated by the cigarette smoke. Right there on the dance floor, I heard God saying to me, "Look at where you are. Suppose something happens to your son and you are not there to take care of him? And is this where I will find you if I return tonight?" Then I started thinking, if I had stayed at home and gone to church with my son the next day, no one would be smoking in the church and even if I had given an offering, it would have been better than spending the money in the club and not being able to enjoy ourselves. I then told my husband that I wanted to go home and he suggested that we go to another club, but I was definitely not interested. Obviously, he was not having all of the same experiences that I was having. That night, I was sure that I heard God calling me loud and clear and I answered him. I actually felt desperate to be in the house of the Lord, so therefore, we went home.

The next day, I communicated with my husband the concerns I had about our son's health and he suggested that we take him to yet another doctor. I said, "Okay, but we need money because we have no insurance." In reply, he said, "If I have to beg, steal, or borrow the money, he will see a doctor." That is when I said, "No! You will not have to beg, steal, or borrow any money. I will take him to church." There were two neighbors next door to me who attended Friday morning services at the same church where I sent my son to Sunday school. In desperation, I called out to them and said that I would like to accompany them to church. My son was feeling a little better on that day and I had already sent him off to school when I made the decision to go. Two days later, he and I went to church. I can still remember how happy he was. After the service, I approached the pastor and tried my best to explain the problem and asked him to pray for my child. Before praying, he asked me if I had taken him to see a doctor and my answer was yes, several doctors who had no answers for me. He laid his hand on my son and prayed a simple prayer over him, and I believed that he was healed. The next day after coming home from school, he said, "Mom, you know the thing happened again." Meaning, the feeling of pulling in his face and slurred speech. With indignation I declared out loud, "No, that was just your imagination. It shall not happen again." Praise the Lord, it has never happened again. God loves us and is always trying to get our attention. He got it through my son. This was truly being led by a child.

⌘

Between the age of seven and eight years old while I was living with my father's relative, I had gone up to the altar after there was an altar call for salvation in a Seventh-day Adventist (SDA)church. Before my parents separated, my mother took my brothers and me also to an SDA church regularly. With all of the instability in my life,

I had moved away from the church. Now that I am older, I think that I must have gone to the altar then out of fear after hearing some of the fire and brimstone messages and not wanting to burn, got the fire insurance, but did not understand at that time the depth of God's love for me.

⚮

I began intensely seeking, searching, fasting, and praying to the point where nothing else mattered. During this next season of my life, there were two church sisters who were very helpful to me. One of them was my next-door neighbor and the other was my house guest. She was having some faith fights of her own and needed a place to stay, which my husband and I provided, but I really do believe that these two incredible women were a gift from God to me. He knows just what we need and when we need it. They were my prayer partners.

At the church where I had quickly become a member, one of the pastors prophesied that God was going to do a quick work in my life for where he was taking me. It sounded good. Ha-ha! And it was good.

> And we know that, all things work together for good to them that love God, to them who are called according to his purpose. (Romans 8:28, KJV)

Love is not love until it is put to the test. Bottomline was, my marriage was in trouble. I learned that fasting and praying would reveal things to you that you cannot see or perceive with your natural senses. Even before I got married, I had made the decision to break the cycle of divorce, separation and broken family relationships prevalent in the maternal side of my family. I just wanted to change the narrative. Generational spirits will always try to inhabit the next generation if someone would let them in. Matthew 8:28–34 tells of Jesus meeting the two demon-possessed men coming out the tombs (dead and unfruitful places, decay, stench, loss, and sorrow) and the demons (tormenting spirits) begging Jesus not to send them out of the area but into the herd of pigs nearby. I think they wanted to stay in that area to inhabit some other unenlightened person or persons.

When my husband and I met and before and after we got married, there were important information and things that I was supposed to know that was withheld by him from me. There were two children that I did not gave birth to who were part of our lives. When I found out, I must confess that I felt betrayed and had a myriad of emotions. Even thoughts of leaving had entered my mind, but when I looked at where I was and where God had brought me from, and wanting to break the generational cycle of divorce and separation not only for myself but for my children and my children's children, I knew in my heart that God had gotten me this far and will see me through. I remember my oldest son who was eleven years old and always an old soul asking me, "Mom, suppose you had found this out before you were a Christian, what would you have done?" My answer was, "When you are a baby, you eat baby food but when you are an adult, you have to eat what is fit for an adult." I knew that it was not the time for me to make rash decisions but to trust God in the process. This must have been a part of the quick work that was prophesied that God was doing in me.

No child is responsible how they arrive into the world. It is by the actions of their parents and the grace of God. Instead of two children, my husband and I are now the proud parents of four adult children and ten grandchildren. I believe that it was good that certain things were revealed to me before migrating to the USA because we were coming to live with my extended family members. There was a lot of work to be done in our relationship but at least the cat was out of the bag. No more secrets.

4

Tithes and Offering

I began hearing the Lord speaking to me clearly and started to act on His word. Because I was the only one of my mother's children who was married at the time, I had to wait until she became an American citizen to sponsor me. All of my other siblings except one had already migrated. I was beginning to learn the power of giving and sowing money seeds after a sister in Christ quoted Malachi 3:10–12 (KJV)

> Bring ye all the tithes in the storehouse, that there may be meat in mine house, and prove me herewith saith the Lord of Host, If I will not open you the windows of heaven, and pour you out a blessing, that there shall not be enough room to receive it.

She also told me that she applies it to her life and God never failed to keep his promises according to His word. I decided to trust Him one more time. The members of the church I attended were challenged to sow a financial seed toward the hosting of a pastor who was coming to minister to us from the Bahamas. I had a few hundred dollars in the bank and decided to give it all. That was the largest money seed that I had ever sown at any time. I began to hear God speaking to me even more clearly than I was hearing him before saying, "The things that you see as obstacles in your life are not obstacles, I have allowed them to be there for your highest good and when I am ready to move you, nothing is going to stop you, not even the seeming lack of money, because there is no lack." In (2 Kings 4:2, KJV) And Elisha said unto her, what shall I do for thee? Tell me, what do you have in the house? And she said, "thy hand-maid hath not anything in the house, save a pot of oil." I would also like to ask, what do you have in your life? We all have something to give. 2 Corinthians 9:10 (KJV) says, "Now he that ministereth seed to the sower both minister bread for your food, and multiply your seed sown, and increase the fruits of your righteousness." What we have may seem insignificant and cannot meet our need, but instead of complaining and worrying about not having enough, look for the opportunity to sow, not grudgingly or haphazardly but with the spirit of excellence and expectation knowing that God is your source and He will lead, guide, and provide. You may not have a job but you can volunteer your time and service as a seed, and in due season you will reap. It is the law of reciprocation.

My maternal grandmother was staying with my family and I in preparation for migration to the USA. During that time, there were very few planes flying in and out of Guyana. The airline that she was going to fly with required that we pay for her ticket with US dollars. My mother had left us some money on one of her visits for that same purpose but during the time of waiting, my husband and I had used some of the money and was unable to replace it on time. Someone had promised to lend it to him but backed out at the last minute: therefore, I challenged him to pray and start thanking God for the money and watch it show up because neither of us had any idea as to where or who we were going to get it from. He came home excited to announce that he did not have to borrow the money because some-one that he did not know personally gave to him the amount of money that he needed. That someone turned out to be the friend of the person he was going to borrow it from. My grandmother got her ticket and was on her way. There were times before when I would tell my husband about the goodness and faithfulness of God and he would tell me that he could not see what I was talking about. Well, a question was asked by a pastor: how do you know that the word of God is true? People were giving all sorts of answers, but the one answer that he was looking for was "because I have experienced it for myself." By this time, I personally had experienced more than enough to allow doubt and unbelief to still dwell in my heart.

I dreamt one night that my family and I were at the airport and ready to leave Guyana but were stopped because we had no income tax clearance required when leaving on a permanent visa. I remembered that God had told me before when he was ready to move me that nothing was going to stop me; therefore, I was not worried. When you are forewarned you are forearmed. While processing our paper work for migration, a situation did show up concerning our taxes. I was a homemaker but my husband was self-employed. He came to me and suggested that we could pay someone to fix it in such a way that we could leave, then pay what was owed later. I did not think that was the route we should have taken, especially after God had told me that nothing was going to stop me when he was ready to move me. I suggested that we pray and trust God's guidance in the process. My sister in Christ who was our house guest overheard us having the discussion and referred us to someone in the income tax office that she knew. We were then instructed by that person how to handle the matter. As we were walking away from her office, I heard a familiar voice asking the question, "Why do you look so sad, sis?" I looked up and it was my adult Sunday school teacher walking toward us. We told him what the issue was, and he said, "Don't worry, I know just the man who can help you." Then he exclaimed, "Here comes the man." Yes, there came the man walking toward us and my husband and the man knew each other. I went on my merry way home and my husband got his income taxes straightened out and was able to get his clearance. After obtaining our visas, we did not have enough money to purchase our tickets, but I started packing our suitcases and emptying our rental home by giving away, selling, and throwing out the stuff that we did not need anymore. I announced to my husband that we would be leaving in one week's time. Most times, people are looking for the signs before they move, but faith without works is dead (James 2:26, KJV). I chose to believe and put action to my faith. I called my mother and told her that we needed $1,000. Without a question, she told me to expect it the next day. I did not know that she had bought a house in preparation for our arrival. If I did, I might have been hesitant to ask her. She kept the purchase of the house a secret because she wanted to surprise me. I found out sometime later that my husband knew but did not say a word. During this season, I was studying the book of Deuteronomy, and I heard God saying to me that He was taking me to a place where I have never been before and I will find things prepared for me that I did not work for or put there. In one week as I prophesied, we arrived in New York City. When we got to my mother's house, she announced, "This is my house. I bought it a month ago." Later on, before she retired, she asked us to take over the house. Here again, I was seeing the manifestation of God as I trusted Him.

My oldest son must have understood the principle of tithing and sowing at a very young age because one day he came to me and said, "Mum, I need a computer and the money I have is not enough to buy one. Therefore, I am sowing it." He received two computers shortly after. One from a scholarship sponsor and the other from his dad. He was able to lend one of his to a schoolmate after hers was giving trouble. My next day in church, the prophet of God said, "Raise your tithe to the Lord and know that whatever you are believing the Lord for, you have it, and a sign shall be even before your feet hit the pavement, the rain will start falling." I did not know what others were believing God for, but I was believing God for my son's safety and protection. That same weekend, he had gone with a group of students to Poughkeepsie. When church was over and I stepped outside, the rain began to fall just as the prophet said, and I knew that I had what I was believing God for, the safety and protection of my son. The next day, I went to work and was walking outdoors with my patient who was also a believer and I drew her attention toward a water fountain by saying, "See that water fountain, it is like when the Holy Spirit is in your life and it is never dry." She agreed. On my way home on the bus, I closed my eyes and went into a meditative state and saw the ocean, a large rock in the middle of the ocean, and a beacon of light on top of the rock in the ocean. Then, I heard the Lord saying to me, "See that water, I am that. See that rock, I am that. See that light, I am that." About fifteen minutes after I got home, the telephone rang and it was the assistant director from the scholarship program, calling to inform me that my son had a near-drowning accident and was in the intensive care unit at the hospital. She was extremely nervous but I was very calm. The question to me was, "Are you coming up to see your son?" My answer was, "No, he is fine and will be out soon." I guess she must have thought, *this woman is in a state of shock and denial.* Well denial, yes! I was denying that anything was wrong with my child after giving my tithe and receiving that word with the evidence of the rain beginning to fall. The only request I made was for him to call me when it was possible to get to a telephone. He did, and the first thing that I said to him was, "Son, you ought to say praise the Lord." His response was, "Mum, that is the first thing I did." His recollection of the event are as follows. He was sitting on the side of the pool while two other kids were horsing around and knocked him over into the pool. He hit his head on the edge of the pool going down and was in the water for quite a while because no one realized he was hurt, also that he did not know how to swim; therefore, no one attempted to pull him out. Thank God one young lady noticed him struggling and summoned help to get him out of the water. By that time, he was unconscious. When he regained consciousness, he said that he saw a light. That surely sounded like the beacon of light, the water and the rock that I saw while in meditation on the bus and God assured me by saying, "I *am* that."

Your tithe will not only cover you but will also cover your household. It is the thing that God will use to rebuke the devourer for your sake. He rebuked the death angel from taking my son's life. Malachi 3:11 (KJV) says, "And I will rebuke the devourer for your sake." God does not need our money because everything belongs to Him. Psalm 24:1–3 (KJV) says, "The earth is the Lord's and the fullness thereof; the world and they that dwell therein." He wants us to believe and trust in Him and not in ourselves. Proverbs 3:5 (KJV) says, "Trust in the Lord with all of our hearts and lean not unto thine own understanding."

5

Transition

Coming to the US was a major change for the entire family. We came as family of four and now had to merge with my extended family members. Less privacy, limited personal belongings, apprehension, mixed emotions, and for me some bitterness and unforgiveness toward my husband and others who I thought had done me wrong. I am not ashamed to say this because it may help someone. You can create a number of diseases in your body by not releasing the past. Man is a spirit that lives in a body and has a soul. I do believe that whatever affects you in your mental and emotional life can affect you in your physical body. I remember being alone one day and was talking to God about my husband and the things that I was unhappy about and I could hear Him talking back to me. Some may ask, does God really speak to you? Yes, God speaks in so many ways, and we can have meaningful conversations with Him. He speaks through people, through the Bible, in our dreams, and in that still small voice that some mistakenly call something. They would say, "Something told me not to do so and so, and I should have listened." You see, God is spirit and we are also spirits created in His image and likeness but just wrapped in flesh. Flesh is our earthly suit. To have a relationship with him or anyone else, we have to speak and communicate or there would be no relationship. Sometimes, the one we speak to the least is the one we need to speak to the most, but that depends on if He is the most important one in our lives as he should be. We need to cultivate the habit of entertaining His presence. He is not limited by the flesh, or time, or space. He is omnipresent. In John 14:26 (KJV), "But the Comforter which is the Holy Ghost, whom the Father will send in my name, he will teach you all things, and bring all things to your remembrance, whatsoever I have said unto you." It will be unwise for us to ignore our help. Now, back to my conversation with Him. He told me to stop looking at my husband and look to him, because what we both needed, we could not give to each other, because there is a place in each person's life that is reserved only for Christ. And when I talk about my husband in a negative way, pointing out his flaws and shortcomings, I am joining forces with hell in pulling him down, and in doing, so I am pulling myself down because the two of us are one. That was an eye opener. Sometimes, the very thing that annoys you in another person's life is the very thing that you need to change. When I took my focus off him and allowed God to work in my life and I changed, he changed. Instead of focusing on the negative, I started to use my words creatively by calling those things that are not as though they were.

There were now four generations under one roof—my maternal grandmother, my mother, my children, and me. There were many spiritual battles, but I fought the good fight of faith and was able to overcome and be victorious by the grace of God, over the generational spirits that my mother and my grandmother had battled in their lives. I believe that God was now giving me the opportunity to establish a new foundation for myself and family. It was really a time of healing and restoration for me, even though I am still a work in progress. There are always opportunities to be offended but you have to ask yourself, what is in me that is causing me to be offended? It may be that there is something in you yet to be healed and you are offended because someone touched your sore spot.

Before leaving Guyana, I had purposed in my heart to find a church where I can grow. An American woman I met in Guyana had given me a telephone number which I thought was her personal number. A few days after I arrived in the US, I called and found out it was a church number and the person I was looking for was no longer a member there. The pastor who answered the phone told me that he was also from Guyana and invited me to visit to see if that was the place where God wanted me to be. On my second visit, he introduced me to a couple who were also from Guyana. Shortly after, they left and went to a church in the city. I wanted to join them but my family could not understand why I was leaving Queens with so many churches around to travel all the way to Manhattan. I've learned that not every place with a sign up claiming to be a church is really a church; it could be just a den of thieves, so I was being very prayerful and cautious.

I was not working at the time. As a matter of fact, I had never worked before. My father took care of me financially up to when I got married and I did not know how to use my own God-given abilities and talents to generate my own income. For me, to even think about travelling to Manhattan to attend church, I had to have some money. I began seeking employment but the two main things that employers would ask for are qualifications and experience. As I mentioned before, with all of the interruptions and dysfunction in my early childhood and young adulthood, I was never able to stay in any place long enough to complete my education. Now, it was quite frustrating not knowing which way to go. My husband was also seeking employment in order to support himself and the family and that was also quite a task, even though he was trained in his field of work in the USA in 1979 when he came on a scholarship. This was also a very rocky period in our relationship, and not having enough money was our biggest issues. I started volunteering to serve at a children's psychiatric hospital with a church sister, and I must say that it was very sad to see after my own experiences where those children were. When you think your situation is bad, there are others in worse situations. I believe that just making a decision to volunteer and not sitting and waiting opened the door to my first job. It was with a family who were very kind to me. The lady of the home was wheelchair bound and needed assistance to get things done in, around, and out of her home. I remember saying to her the first time we met that I would appreciate it if she would let me know how she would like to have things done because my way may not be her way. She responded by saying, "Honey, however you do it your home, do it in mine." I stayed there for about a year and it was a very pleasant experience for me. I do believe that it was so because before I migrated to the USA, I had people come into my home to work for me and I treated them fairly. "Whatsoever a man soweth that shall he also reap" (Galatians 6:7, KJV). Every other place that I worked after that I met Mrs. Bitterness, Mrs. Unforgiveness, and Mrs. Bewilderment. I was meeting those people because they represented other areas of my life that still needed to be redeemed.

I had left the first church that I attended after I came to the US and found a smaller church in my neighborhood. I quickly became involved in ministry and started out being a Sunday school teacher to becoming the Sunday school superintendent, a choir member, and a worship group leader; but I must admit that I could not get the church in the city out of my mind. I would visit occasionally and must have read all of the books and teaching material that I could get my hands on. I was beginning to feel stagnated where I was and desperately hungry for more. One of the things that I did not understand was whenever it was time for the tithes and offering, why the pastor would almost be apologizing for challenging the people to give. I guess one other person felt the same way because she spoke up and said, "Pastor, Deuteronomy 25:4 (KJV) says, 'Do not muzzle the ox that tresheth the corn.'" She also quoted Malachi 3:8–11. Some may say that God was speaking to those people then and that don't apply to us now, but God is the same yesterday, today, and forever; and I rather trust the one who knows it all. I know that we are the church, but where we congregate as a local body, bills have to be paid just like anywhere else, and it is only right if the man or woman of God should dedicate themselves to studying, teaching, preaching, and contributing to the prosperity of your souls that you should want to reciprocate in any way you can. According to 1 Corinthians 9:11 (KJV), "If we have sown spiritual things unto you, is it a great thing if we shall reap your carnal things."

I do believe the preachers job is to teach and preach the word of God without apology and reservation and to give the people the opportunity to respond according to their faith. The challenge was not there, and I was beginning to feel like I was under a closed heaven. I was desperate for change and growth and to see the promises of God manifested in my life. Even some of the songs that was being sung sounded unscriptural to me. For example: "I don't need a million dollars, don't need a pot of gold" but yet praying that God would bless financially surely did not make sense to me. I started sneaking over to the other church and was accompanied by a young man who had just left Bible school in Barbados and was seeking a pastor to mentor him. He accompanied me one day, and as fate would have it, they were filming and we were caught on camera and seen on TV by my current pastor. He approached us and asked what did we know about the pastor of that church, and I am sure it was out of genuine concern for our souls. I had already started to feel divided in my loyalty and knew that I had to make a decision to stop straddling the fence, so I wrote a letter of resignation thanking the man of God for all that he had imparted in my life, also letting him know that I felt it was my time to go. He called me up and tried to convince me to stay by suggesting that I cancel my decision and be in church the next day, but what made me want to go faster was when he asked me what did I think was going to happen to the other believers when I leave, and that bothered me. I did not have a discussion with any other member of the church concerning my decision to leave. The only other person who knew that I was leaving was the young man from Barbados who was searching for someone to mentor him. That place, the pastor, and his lovely family was a blessing to me and my family and will be a blessing to others, but one cannot remain in the same class all of their lives, and I personally needed to catch up. We are designed for growth and I needed to be fed, but I certainly was not disgruntled. Sad to say, shortly after I left, the man of God passed away. I cannot explain it and would not even try.

It was around this time that my husband had found receipts of my giving to other ministries where I was gleaning from and being blessed. He told my mother that he was leaving because I was giving my money away. I have come to realize that when any one has a problem with giving money it is really not about the money, it is about their life and time. After all, that is the two things that you give in exchange for this thing you call "money." I was hungry for spiritual food and I gave something to get something. I was making room in my life to receive. Needless to say, he did leave, and this provoked me to sow a larger seed into the prophetic ministry where I felt that God was leading me to. I did not say anything to the man of God but he prophesied, saying that he felt peace concerning my marriage, and as I continue to become kind in my own heart, God was going to open up things in my home. He also said that he saw a little boy, one of my sons, who was going to grow up to become a man of strength. I went home and did not feel the need to pray but just to praise God. I told my children that their father will be home in three days, and like I said, in three days he came home to a kind and loving wife and a warm meal. On that same day, our oldest son received a scholarship of $23,500 in the mail. He was attending a boarding school at the time. For the four years that he was at the school, he received a total of about $80,000 in scholarship. I was also blessed to have my airfare, limousine, and accommodations taken care of. This was absolutely the favor of God. You cannot beat God's giving no matter how hard you try. Giving is our heavenly father's nature; therefore, giving must be our nature and way of life.

6

Where Is My Wealth?

From the time I gave my heart to the Lord, my understanding was everything that I had lost through separation from God will be restored. One of my favorite scripture verses is 3 John 1-2 (KJV) "Beloved, I wish above all things that thou mayest prosper and be in health, even as thy soul prospereth." Some people think of prosperity and wealth only in terms of having a lot of money and material goods, but God's kind of prosperity concerns every area of our lives. Webster dictionary defines it as "a flourishing state; satisfactory progress and success." I know of some who won large sums of money by playing the lottery but because of the poorness of their soul (mind, will, and emotions), they lost it all, and their lives ended up being in a worse condition than before they acquired the money. Some people are very educated and legitimately worked and acquired lots of money, but there again, that may be all that they have, just lots of education and money but poor in soul. We have seen some so-called celebrities who have used their talents and became famous had a lot of money and material goods but passed on too soon because of the neglect of their souls. For some, if they have it and unfortunately lose it, they literally end their lives because losing their money is like losing their god. It is a blessing to be wealthy and prosperous. More to give, more to sow, more to enjoy, and more to meet our needs.

But Jesus answered him saying, "Man shall not live by bread alone, but by every word of God." (Luke 4:4, KJV)

For what shall it profit a man to gain the whole world and lose his own soul? (Mark 6:36, KJV)

If as a believer in Christ you lose it all, you can recreate it again because you know where that came from there is more. Our God is a God of endless supply.

But thou shalt remember the Lord thy God: for it is he that giveth thee power to get wealth that he may establish his covenant which he swore unto thy fathers, as it is this day. (Deuteronomy 8:18, KJV)

Many are seeking money and material gain which is okay, but once you come into the wealth of wisdom, knowledge, and understanding of the principles laid out by Almighty God in His word and begin to exercise your faith, working diligently toward accomplishing your goals and dreams, eventually, it will manifest in your experience. As a child, I wanted to be a poet, an artist, a writer, and a beautician. Before leaving Guyana, I told my mother that I wanted to enroll in cosmetology school when I got to the US. Well, she talked me out of it by telling me if I messed up anyone's hair, they were going to sue me. Now I know that was not intentional, but it did put a fear in my heart and turned me off from going forward with it. After doing multiple jobs over the years and feeling unfulfilled, the desire for cosmetology school resurfaced but I had a number of excuses why I could not do it, and the main one was that I did not have the money. How quickly we forget after all God had done for us. I was working as a home health aide at the time, and I observed the way my client would sit in her wheelchair all day long, even though she could walk and move around without it. This was a very talented lady who did excellent artwork that was marketable, but she just sat in her wheel-chair and complained about her past, present, and future. I heard God saying to me, "What a wicked servant and that is you. I have given you power to get wealth and there you are complaining about what you do not have." Someone said, "To get something you do not have, you have to do something you've never done." I had to put action to my faith. A sister in Christ so wanted me to succeed that she went about gathering the information of cosmetology schools for me. I talked about it so much that even my husband began telling me not to worry about money. I remember Prophet Manasseh Jordan as a little boy about six to seven years old standing next to me in church one day looked straight in my face and said, "That thing that you are believing God for you better reach down into yourself and pull it up." I knew exactly what he was talking about, and that was the voice of God through the mouth of that child.

Here again I was given the opportunity to exercise my faith. You can stand in front of a door with a sensor saying open sesame, but that door will never open until you walk toward it. Eventually, I stepped out in faith and signs followed me. I went to school full time, and the same day I graduated, I got a job in a beauty salon even before obtaining my license. There, I met a lovely young lady named Loretta who introduced me to the entertainment industry to do both hair and make-up on movie sets, theater, commercials, and music videos. During this season, I was now a full-time member at Zoe Ministries, and the teaching in this place was challenging me to grow up into the life that God had ordained for me to walk into. I was now working daily on eliminating ideas and mindsets that was not beneficial to my growth and well-being. A little while after I became a cosmetologist, I met a young lady at a friend's house, and she asked me if I was in the medical field. My answer to her question was "No, I am a cosmetologist." Her response to that was "No, not doing hair," with the look on her face as if I said a dirty word. She said that I spoke as someone who was knowledgeable of the medical field and was trying to convince me to go and do medical billing because she told someone else who was a hairstylist to go into the same field and that person became successful. Well, I must say, had

I gone into the medical field, it would definitely not be for medical billing but for hands on interaction with the patients. The lady of the house then asked her, "What if she likes what she is doing?" After a little while, the young lady and I were left alone in the room because our host became busy in the kitchen. She came over where I was sitting and stooped down next to my chair and started talking to me in a low tone because she did not want the young man that she came with hear what she was saying to me. He was in another part of the house with my husband and the man of the house watching a football game on TV. She started telling me without my asking all about her life. She was married, but the man she came to the house with was not her husband, and she did not know who she wanted to be with. I then asked her about her relationship with her father and she started crying. Her father is a pastor and her being the oldest of three girls had to keep her younger sisters in line when they were all children, and if she did not, the consequences were physical chastisement by her father, which made her very angry and resentful toward him. I was then able to show her why she was having so many problems with the men in her life and her ability in making the right choices. I led her into a prayer of forgiveness of her father. After that, she was not trying to convince me anymore to go into the medical field but to keep on doing what I was doing. I have come to realize that God has given us gifts, talents, and abilities but those gifts, talents, and abilities are not just for us. God in his wisdom made no man self-sufficient or as some would say, no man is an island. Everyone was given something to contribute and to serve in the human experience as a whole, and we should serve people the way we desire to be served. Luke 6:31(KJV) says, "And as ye would that men should do to you, do ye also to them likewise." No matter what is your status in life, one should not think too highly about themselves nor should they think of themselves as a worm. James 1:17 (KJV) also says, "Every good and perfect gift is from above, and cometh down from the Father of lights, with whom is no variableness neither shadow of turning." Our gifts, talents, and abilities do not always come wrapped in pretty packages, but are sometimes hidden and then revealed through the experiences we have in our lives. No one made the decision as to where, when, time, and place they were going to be born, their ethnicity, the color of their skin, or what the educational and socio-economic status of their parents were going to be, and that is why one should never look down upon another unless you are willing to give that person who may be in a less fortunate situation than yourself a hand up. Being formally and informally educated is important in order to be effective in any particular area of service. By all means celebrate your accomplishments. I serve as a cosmetologist and that does not make my area of service any more or less important than anyone else's, as some may imply. You may ask, why did I name the book *Healing Hands*? Well, by using my hands to enhance the beauty of the hair and faces of my clients, I sometimes get the opportunity while they are sitting under my hands in my chair to use that chair as a pulpit to minister to their souls, pulling them out of the mental and emotional dark pits they sometimes find themselves in and not by beating them over their heads with the Bible, but just in conversation and sharing my testimonies of what God has done in my life. In times past, I felt like I was in a pit, but now I know that God was always with me even in the darkest times of my life and is here with me now. I remember one person saying to me that I did not understand what she was going through because I appear to be someone who grew up with a silver spoon in my mouth. Well, for her to see me that way is a beautiful thing. God must have done and is doing a wonderful work in my life. When I shared my story with her, she said it gave her hope.

7

The Grasshopper Complex

On a very late night after leaving one of our church conferences, which was being held in a NYC hotel to go home—and home for me was two trains and a cab or bus ride away—I left resenting the fact I could not stay for the night at the hotel like others were, also because I had no extra money to give an offering. I walked to the train station, and when I got to the top of the stairs, I slipped and fell and had to hold on to the nearest rail for dear life with one hand. No one was around to give me a hand up. By the grace of God, I managed to pull myself up and was in excruciating pain. Right away, I realized why I fell. I heard that still small voice inside of me saying, "You were thinking like a grasshopper and not like a giant. Because you were thinking low, your body had to follow. The pain in my arm and leg reminded me for a long time to keep my mind stayed on the Lord.

8

Get Your Self-esteem Off the Seesaw

Sometime in 1997, I came home from work feeling physically and mentally tired. I was trying to manage work, family, and church and felt overwhelmed. When I got in the door, someone was on TV talking about keeping a gratitude journal by writing at least five things that you were grateful for every day, and on the days that you were not feeling so good, to go back and look at the things that you had previously written to encourage yourself. Well, I started writing and counted thirty-five things. I am sure that I could have remembered and written more had I continued. The next day, on my way home from work I found myself meditating on God is love. I've heard and said those words numerous times, but this time it had new meaning for me. I came to the realization of not only that He is love, but He also lives in me. He created me. He is the essence of my being. Without Him, there would be no me. Therefore, I will never feel unloved or unfulfilled again because I am God's love in expression, and I do not have to look outside of myself for love again. One can be desperately searching outside of themselves for their good, looking to another person or thing, but that will only lead to a place of more emptiness. There is a place in each human being that is reserved only for Almighty God.

And when he was demanded of the Pharisees when the kingdom of God would come, he answered them and said, the Kingdom of God cometh not with observation:(21) Neither shall they say, Lo here! Lo there! for behold, the kingdom of God is within you. (Luke 17:20–21, KJV)

Not going into the secret place will leave you longing, wandering, and wishing. Once you come to that realization, you will never blame anyone again for your shortcomings.

9

My Mother, My Friend

My earliest memory of my mother was very vague. As stated before, I was only three years old when my parents separated, but what I do remember were her beautiful hats, shoes, and clothing she left behind. I would play dress up and pretend to be her. I knew that she lived in the city, and I missed her so much. I asked my father to let me go and visit her at Christmas time, but he told me that she was dead. That was not the appropriate thing to say to a child or children, especially if it was not the truth. A lot of people took the pleasure of telling me how rotten my mother was for abandoning my siblings and me, but now that I've grown and have experienced life, I know that she is truly a remarkable woman who refused to be treated in a way that was unacceptable to her. That was her God-given right and she did something about it. She left. Only the one who feels the pain knows the pain. Yes, our family was fragmented and we all had our share of troubles, but thanks be to God, we do not have to live in the past. The rest of our lives can be the best of our lives, and I intend, by the grace of God, to make it so.

10

The Wise Use of Money

(Money Management Skills)

My father worked for lumber companies, trucking, and building roads in the interior of the country and he was paid large sums of money. Many people told my brothers and me that the amount of money he worked for he could have bought the whole village. Daddy was generous and too freehanded with some people, had a lot of friends, made some bad business deals, and many times he was defrauded. Whenever I was around, he would give me money to get anything and everything that my little heart desired and always admonished me not to accept anything from anyone, but too much too soon was not good. After I got married, I depended on my husband like I depended on my father and did not realize it until much later. Some very negative circumstances made me woke up to who really is my source. After I started working and handling my own money, I also did not know how to use it wisely. I was and am a tither, sower, and giver, but yet I had a large credit card debt, which caused me much worry. At times, I really felt like a slave to the lender. Nothing in life is for free. Credit card debt has taught me a lesson and I paid the price for it. Now, I no longer call it a debt but an investment in my money management education of the wise use of money. I appreciate it for it has taught me something that I did not know before. It is important to look at life from both sides. If you only look at the side that was seemingly negative and not look for the lesson or lessons that you can learn, which may save you from repeating the same mistakes, then the price you paid would all have been in vain. Learning to change your perception could be the best thing you ever do for yourself. I am glad to say that I no longer have any large and unmanageable credit card debt.

11

Are You Eclipsing Your Growth by Your Thinking?

Several years ago, I took the pleasure of cutting off my shoulder-length hair in exchange for an Afro hairdo. After a while, I made several attempts to grow it back but would just cut it off again. When anyone would ask why did I cut my hair again, my answer would be because I do not like the in-between stage and there was nothing much that I could do with it. I did this repeatedly which was insane. I began to notice a little cyst at the side of my head and it was sometimes painful. Every time I combed my hair or whenever my barber would use his clippers on the side of my head to maintain my hairstyle, it would become inflamed, so I decided to pay my doctor a visit. While I was in the waiting room, I decided to take out a book from my bag that I was reading. The author stated that whenever boils and fever and other diseases manifest in the body, it may be because you have been harboring some ungodly thought in the mind that you need to let go of. We are encouraged in Philippians 2:5 (KJV) to "let this mind be in you that is also in Christ. Think it not robbery to be equal with God (2:6)." Also, in Proverbs 23:7 (KJV), it says, "As a man thinketh in his heart, so is he. I began to check myself to see if there was yet something that I needed to get rid of, and I remembered looking into an old briefcase where I kept important papers the day before and seeing an envelope containing the hair that I had cut off my head so very long ago. Obviously, I was keeping it because I had attached some kind of sentimental value to it. At times, I would look at it and say to myself, "Look how long my hair used to be." One can get so focused on what was, that they cannot see what is. After arriving home from the doctor's office, I heard the Lord speaking to me. He was encouraging me to take the envelope containing my hair that I was holding on to and flush it down the toilet. I then realized that the hair represented all of the negative, erroneous, fearful, and limiting thoughts I once had. God showed me where I had cut off those thoughts by renewing my mind in the washing of His word, but like a gardener who had cut off the wild and overgrown bushes but did not take up the dead stuff and put it in the trash, so was I with my hair. I had allowed dead things to take up valuable space in my life and was eclipsing my growth. Once I released and flushed those thoughts into the sea of forgetfulness, my head was healed and my hair began to grow beautifully.

12

Is There Room in You for the Christ Child?

Psalm 91:1 (KJV) says, "He that dwelleth in the secret place of the Most High shall abide under the shadow of the Almighty." God is saying, "Come into the secret place that I may overshadow you, even as Mary was overshadowed by the Holy Ghost and was impregnated with the son of God. Know that the secret place is a place of perfect love and intimacy which eliminates all fear. This is the place where you can tell the Lord of your life, a.k.a. the love of your life, your most secret desires and He will tell you His. He is not a man who should lie or make empty promises to you. He is omnipotent and can deliver according to His word. All you have to do is believe and receive the seed that He has deposited in your spirit, but you must guard it lest the enemies of your soul, which is doubt and unbelief, cause you to abort it.

In due season, you will give birth or manifest that which the Holy Ghost had impregnated you with. The secret place is a place of agreement. What God has joined together let no man (mind) put asunder. The child that Mary was pregnant with was not by her man, Joseph. He wanted to put her away. This let me know that the closest person to you may not always understand but only those who have an ear to hear what the Spirit is saying. When God is doing a work in you, He will cover you on every side, but the key is staying in the secret place. When it is time for you to manifest and bring forth that

49

which is not man's doing but God's doing, men will see His good works in and through your life and will be drawn unto Him.

Once you have given birth to that which you were pregnant with, you can go on and continue to be fruitful and multiply. If you do it once, you can do it again. Refusing to go into the secret place and coming into oneness with "I AM" is the cause of sin and separation from God's highest good for your life.

Choose ye this day which way you may go.
(Joshua 24:15, KJV)

13

It Shall Cost You

When I made up my mind to step out of mediocrity and began to earnestly seek to fulfill God's will for my life, I did not know where it was going to take me. I was misunderstood by family members who thought that I had lost my mind and was even accused of infidelity because of my church attendance. This just let me know that I was on the right track. Jesus the master himself was wrongfully accused, spat upon, beaten, and killed. There were others in the Bible and there will be more who will experience the same fate, so one is never alone. I had made a conscious decision to let go of self and not let what man think, say, or do derail me from my goal and God's will for my life. There can be no resurrection without death, and without darkness there can be no light. For Christ to be seen in your life, a crucifixion must take place. The world expects you to go under if you do not conform to their way of thinking, and they may even quote scripture to you to tell you all of the reasons why you should not be doing what you are doing based on their understanding. That is the time for you to affirm the word in your own life and be encouraged, knowing that God will not fail you. The determining factor should not be what you hear, feel, smell, taste, or see; but your walk with God should be based on truth—what the Lord is saying in His word concerning you. The beautiful thing about life is that God gave each man a measure of faith and it is up to you to demonstrate your faith, regardless of anyone else's belief or objections. That is your God-given right.

God may say things to you that you cannot utter to another and if you do tell it, you leave yourself open to ridicule and scorn. Like Joseph, you may end up in places that you never dreamed of, but let time spent in that place be a time of coming into oneness with God. Avoid becoming bitter and unforgiving toward those who might have inflicted you and caused you pain out of ignorance of what God was and is doing in and through your life. Look out for those who would try to rip God's robe of righteousness off you to put you back in filthy rags or seduce you away from fulfilling your destiny. Bottomline is, if anyone is trying to get you to doubt your faith in God, run for your life, but run into God. Proverbs 18:10 (KJV) says, "The name of the Lord is a strong tower, the righteous run into it and they are saved." Eventually, you will go from the pit to the palace or from training to reigning but know that even your adversaries had their part to play in getting you there. Matthew 5:44–45 (KJV) says, "But I say unto you, Love your enemies, bless them that curse you, and do good to them that hate you, and pray for them which despitefully use you and persecute you, That ye may be the children of your Father which is in heaven: for He maketh the sun to rise on the evil and on the good, and sendeth rain on the just and on the unjust." In Luke 23:34 (KJV), Then Jesus said, "Father, forgive them; for they know not what they do." We have to extend the same grace that God has extended toward us.

14

Children Live What They Learn, but I Am No Longer a Child

One evening while I was sitting in a class at church, an instructor reprimanded me for not being able to answer a question that she asked. The words that she used took me back, way back to grade school, even high school years when teachers had said the same words to me that was painful then, and the pain had resurfaced after all that time. I did not know that it was still there. This incident reminded me of Bishop Jordan saying to me that I have the ability to get things started but never able to finish. I must admit that I felt very small in a room full of adults after what the instructor said to me. I left there that evening asking myself why did I feel that way. At least I knew that if there were not something in me to identify with what she said, I would not have felt the way I did. After doing some soul searching, I discovered the reason why I had a hard time completing what I started. It was because of much shifting and moving from place to place as a minor that I did not stay long enough in one place or school to graduate before moving to another home and another school.

The lack of confidence and self-criticism and wanting people's approval had always been my biggest challenges. I went back and thanked the instructor for what she said and how she said it because I was able to rid myself of that hindrance. If I wasn't sitting under that kind of teaching, I might have reacted differently, but I knew better to check myself. I had to go back a couple of years to bring correction into my life. The only way up is down. If the foundation is not solid, the whole structure can be unbalanced. If someone offends you, take the time to look within yourself and see if there is anything that you need to work on. Your blessing can come in any form, even in the form of a seemingly harsh word or criticism.

15

How Do You See Yourself?

This chapter is dedicated to one of my former Sunday school teachers:
Brother Lincoln Joseph.

Do you see yourself poor?
Or do you see yourself rich?
Do you see yourself as a chicken?
Or do you see yourself as an eagle?
Do you see yourself as a failure?
Or do you see yourself as more than a conqueror?
Do you see yourself as a victim?
Or do you see yourself victorious?
Do you see yourself barren?
Or do you see yourself filled with the fulness of God.
Do you see yourself as a pygmy?
Or do you see yourself as a giant?
Do you see yourself impotent?
Or do you see the omnipotence of God?
Do you see yourself lonely?
Or do you see the omnipresence of God?
Do you see yourself ignorant?
Or do you see the omniscience of God? (MGC)

Unless you see yourself as God sees you, you will never become what God wants you to become nor will you accomplish what God wants you to accomplish. So right now, begin to see yourself as God sees you—perfect, whole, complete, and divine (Lincoln Joseph).

16

Finding Balance

I had gotten so busy doing and serving in the church that I was neglecting other areas of my life. The best way that I can describe it is while working at the Brooklyn Academy of Music and hearing a song from a musical play being sung, "My soul is empty and I'm thirsty and dry, it's a long, long way to the river." I was not hearing the voice of God for myself anymore and that put me in a very sad place. I knew that I had to make changes especially as a married woman

> But I would have you without carefulness. He that is unmarried careth for the things that belong to the Lord, how he may please the Lord: But he that is married careth for the things that are of the world, how he may please his wife. There is a difference between a wife and a virgin. The unmarried woman careth for the things of the Lord, that she may be holy both in body and in spirit: but she that is married careth for the things of the world how she may please her husband. (1 Corinthians 7: 32–34, KJV)

Sometimes because of the distance I was getting home in the wee hours of the morning while my husband was asleep, I now see why I was accused of infidelity. Most of the time, I got a ride home with a sister who lived in the neighborhood or I took the railroad and a cab. Many times, on our way home, I had to keep her from falling asleep while she was driving. She was a daycare provider and her days were long. I knew that I had to make changes, therefore I spent a whole day in my room on the floor crying out to God and seeking His presence. He began to show me that I was like the dog with a bone in his mouth crossing the bridge over the brook. He saw his shadow and did not recognize it was the shadow of himself, but thought it was another dog. He opened his mouth to get the other dog's bone, and in doing so, his bone fell out into the brook. Moral of the story: I was chasing shadows. I dropped my bone (word) and was left wanting. Hebrews 10:25 (KJV) says, "Not forsaking the assembling of ourselves together, as the manner of some is: but exhorting one another: and so much the more, as ye see the day approaching." I was assembling myself, but I was neglecting personal time spent with the Lord and with my family that could have led to a whole host of other issues. I had to lose my way to find my way, but I know that my service was not in vain. It may have been easier if my husband and I were serving or attending the same church as a couple. I said to him one day that I know he could not understand the things I was doing then, spending so much time in church, but he must admit that he has a better wife after all. To that he said yes. I am happy to say, we now attending church as a couple. We cannot thank God enough for the way that He has blessed and preserved our marriage and even for our personal growth. May our lives be an inspiration to our children grandchildren, family, friends, and loved ones as they navigate through life, fighting the good fight of faith and knowing that with God, they will always win if they faint not.

17

Family or Foe

This last chapter is dedicated to family.

A few months ago, while viewing a social media sight, I saw a video of two hyenas locked in a fierce battle. It seemed as though not one of them was going to give up, but were going to fight to the end. They were so focused on each other that they could not see the lion who was in plain sight a little way off salivating to eat his next meal. There was also an impala in the opposite direction of the lion that saw the fighting hyenas and the lion. The alert impala saw when the lion began moving in their direction and got out of there in a flash, but the two hyenas was caught off guard by the lion who then ate one of them for dinner.

> Be sober, be vigilant: because your adversary
> the devil, as a roaring lion, walketh about seeking
> whom he may devour. 1 Peter: 8 (KJV)

He goes in search of; in quest of; to try to obtain (Merriam Webster). Most of the time, people—no, not people, I would rather say family—fight each other because they want to win an argument. It is quite all right to have a difference of opinion because we are unique in our own way and will not always see eye to eye. Friction is inevitable in relationships, but we can agree to disagree without becoming mortal enemies. Romans 3:23 (KJV) says, "For all have sinned, and come short (fail to meet standards or expectations) of the glory of God." In other words, not perfect. After Adam and Eve sinned, imperfection was passed on to us, but yet we look for perfection in each other. We are all a work in progress and it is not our job to fix anyone. Allow God to have His perfect way in us.

Two of a kind were fighting, two hyenas. They belonged to the hyena family. We belong to the human family as a whole that is made up of smaller units of families. What would life be like without family? When we do not love and care for the family that God has blessed us with, we are dishonoring our Heavenly Father and exposing ourselves to the onslaught of the enemy. Sometimes, you may want to throw up your hands up and not be bothered, but we are admonished in John 4:7–8 (KJV), "Beloved let us love one another, for love is of God and everyone that loveth is born of God. He that loveth not, Knoweth not God for God is love." To know Him is to be in relationship with Him. One cannot claim to love God and be in relationship with Him and still hold on to grudges, bitterness, anger, and resentment toward others, especially those who are our family members. According to 1 John 4:20 (KJV), "If a man say, I love God, and hateth his brother, he is a liar; for he that loveth not his brother whom he hath seen, how can he love God whom he hath not seen?" If you do not (know) this kind of love that I am talking about, I want to introduce you to Him today.

> For God so loved the world, that he gave his only begotten Son, that whosoever believeth in him should not perish, but have everlasting life. (John 3:16, KJV)

If you were saved and not as loving in the past, ask God to help you to love as He loves unconditionally.

*Original poems
from my Rivers of
Life collection*

Do You Know Who I AM?

I AM
The very essence of your being
Your existence
Your awareness
Can you feel me in the giving and taking of your breath?
I AM present…omnipresent
Can you see me in all of my creation?
Can you give me glory?
Can you hear me, ever speaking?
Be still…listen to my still small voice
Your first thought…it is I
Beckoning you to come a little closer
Draw closer to me and I will draw closer to you
To tell you the secrets of my heart
I desire no more outer court meetings
But an inner court relationship
I long for you to give birth to my plan
Come my beloved, fear not
What I AM about to show you
You may not understand
But know it's all in the power of my hand
Who do you say I AM?

Wake Up Thou That Sleepest

Wake up thou that sleepest
And know that I AM
The mighty one of Israel
That crumbled the tower of Babel
I hear your voice and your questions
I AM the answer to your call
I AM supreme over life's enemies
I have defeated them all
March on with purpose
In the singleness of heart
Your victory was guaranteed
Right from the start.

(12/6/98)

What I Be Is Up to Me

What I be
Is up to me
To live in the flesh
Or divinity
In Harmony with my King, my God
Rooted and grounded in his word
That I may grow up in Him and bear fruit
That's good and fit for the master's use.

Life's Pathways

Walking on life's pathways
Is not always an easy task
But God promised to uphold, lead, and guide you
And you shall be lost
He is all of wisdom
Keep your trust in Him
His word is a sure foundation
Just stand, pray
And you shall win
You may pass through times of uncertainty
Or your vision may be dim
Your destination may even appear to be longer
But press on, keep going
Do not give in.
God will certainly reward you
And take you to a place of rest
After all, where you've been and done
You will discover, it was only a test.

(7/23/99)

Indecision

Why wait in indecision
And not do all you can today?
This moment, this hour, this second
Is not here to stay
Listen to your first thought
God is always right
Waiting for a second one
Will produce a fight
Why wait?
Demonstrate.

(Inspired by Sis Cyrilene Moulton)

Deep Rivers

The river runs deep
Spirit never sleeps
Alive in me
Arise in me
Abide in me
My body is nothing
Unless in you I keep
Oh, Holy Spirit
Holy is your word
When I get silent before you
That's when you can be heard.

My Love Song

I praise you
Magnify you
Exalt your holy name
You are worthy
I adore you
Forever you will reign
My Jesus, my savior
Lover of my soul
You quench my thirst
Again and again
And keeps me asking for more.

Awesome God

Lord, when I look
At where I am today
And what You've brought me through
I know that there is not one thing
That my God, you cannot do
The flesh is just the flesh
without the spirit of life within
And it is a cosmic impossibility
To think the two can be separate
Which is really sin
For wherever I am
God is always there
I will live in victory
And never succumb to fear.

God's Beautiful Black Child

I am God's beautiful Black child
Whether you agree or not
But knowing who my father is
Does mean a whole lot
Thoughts I had about myself
Had caused me not to see
The potential I have within
That God has invested in me
Now I remember who I am
And knowing that I am free
Nothing could ever stop me now
From fulfilling my destiny
Look out world
Here I come
I am God's beautiful Black child
Happy birthday to me.
(God blessed the day I was born)

About the Author

Marilyn Diane Grenion C. was born in Bartica, Essequibo River, Guyana, South America, aka the Land of Many Waters. She is the mother of two biological children, two stepchildren, grandmother of ten grandchildren and married to her loving and supportive husband, Dudley, for thirty-seven years and counting after knowing him for six years.

She accepted Jesus Christ as her Lord and Savior at the tender age of eight years old but backslid as a teenager. She rededicated her life back to the Lord in her early twenties after a series of traumatic events in her life and the life of her first-born son.

She and her family migrated to the USA in 1990 and resides in Queens, New York. Before migrating to the United States, she attended Central Assemblies of God in Georgetown, Guyana. She is a prayer warrior, loves to share the gospel of Jesus Christ and loves and to encourage others with her testimony of healing and restoration. She is also an avid reader, a poet, and now writer of her first book and aspires to write many more.

Marilyn was also trained in the Prophetic at Zoe Ministries in Manhattan, New York City. She and her family currently attend Christian Cultural Center in Brooklyn New York. She is also a licensed cosmetologist and uses her chair not only to enhance the beauty of her clients' hair and faces but also as a pulpit to sometimes help pull them out of the dark places that they may find themselves in by sharing her own testimony of what the Lord has done in her life.

CPSIA information can be obtained
at www.ICGtesting.com
Printed in the USA
LVHW042303201020
669275LV00005B/95